Suggestions for a Weekly Spelling Program

Monday
- Write the Word List on the chalkboard or chart paper.
- Read the Word List together as a class; say and spell each word as a class.
- Identify and discuss the specific spelling element of the lesson.
- Distribute copies of the Word List or have the students copy the list.
  If you elect to have the students copy the list, be sure to check each student's paper to ensure that he/she will be studying the correct spelling of each word.
- Talk about the meaning of each word. The teacher or students may provide definitions or sentences that indicate the meaning of each word.
- Make a list of "special words". The teacher may provide words taken from units under study, or the student may make an individual list of the words that he/she wants to learn.
  Note: Systematically repeat frequently misspelled words.

Tuesday
- Do one of the Fun Spelling Activities suggested on page 43.
- Have students write the spelling words in sentences.

Wednesday
- Review the Word List. Work in pairs. Each takes a turn saying the words as the other spells the words aloud or writes the words.
- Distribute copies of the worksheet for each student to complete. If you choose, have students write their "special" words on the back of the worksheet or attach a separate piece of paper.

Thursday
- Do the writing activity suggested at the bottom of the worksheet. Encourage students to use as many words as possible from the Word List. Feel free to present an alternate writing activity or allow the student to select a topic about which he/she would like to write.

Friday
- Administer a test of the basic Word List. Have the students work in pairs to administer a test of the list of their own "special" words.
- Add a "challenge" segment to the weekly Word List test by dictating and having the students write . . .
  –words that rhyme with those on the basic Word List.
  –simple sentences.
  Use this activity as an opportunity to review and reinforce the correct use of capital letters and punctuation marks. Have students proofread each sentence. If they have omitted capitals or punctuation marks, they are to erase and correct any such error at this time.

List of suggested materials to have ready for use with the Fun Spelling Activities on page 43.

- letter cards: 3" x 5" index cards on which letters of the alphabet have been written. **Note:** Make several extra cards with the vowels and frequently used letters written on them.
- plastic, rubber or wooden letters of the alphabet
- individual chalkboards, chalk and erasers
- markers, crayons, paints and paintbrushes, easel
- typewriter and/or computer
- tape recorder
- yarn, string, pipe cleaners
- butcher paper
- rice, beans, macaroni, seeds, cereal pieces, unpopped popcorn
- glue
- clay

Start the Engine!

Say the name of each picture. Circle the letter that you hear at the beginning. Then write the letter on the line.

Name _____

t n r k y q b d
m g w f l v z
h p j c s

 h t
__ __ __

 n q
__ __ __

 d b
__ __ __

 j g
__ __ __

 n t
__ __ __

 v z
__ __ __

 t r
__ __ __

 m n
__ __ __

 f v
__ __ __

 s c
__ __ __

 j g
__ __ __

 r l
__ __ __

 l p
__ __ __

 z s
__ __ __

 k d
__ __ __

 r w
__ __ __

 c t
__ __ __

 y w
__ __ __

 d b
__ __ __

 n m
__ __ __

Say the name of each picture. Then write the letter that makes the beginning sound.

 ___ acket

 ___ oat

 ___ og

 ___ itt

 ___ ipper

 ___ ock

 ___ an

 ___ icket

 ___ opcorn

 ___ et

 ___ arn

 ___ uilt

 ___ ot dog

 ___ at

 ___ ug

 ___ ock

 ___ atch

 ___ ey

 ___ ap

 ___ an

IF5083 Spelling

Last Stop

Say the name of each picture. Circle the letter that makes the ending sound. Then write the letter on the line.

STATION

 f g

 n p

x b

r b

d l

 p r

b k

l n

t f

 n m

m p

f l

s g

Letters: s d k g t b f l m n r p x

Say the name of each picture. Write the letter that makes the ending sound.

 ca ___   pi ___   be ___   pai ___   ga ___

 duc ___   ja ___   si ___   su ___   ha ___

 roo ___   dru ___   ma ___

Let's Write! On a separate sheet of writing paper, write sentences about what you might see out the window while riding on a train.

Tangled Taffy

Name _____

Word List

cap   mat   pan

sat bat jam   fat   van

Write the word that names each picture.

Write the two words that did not have pictures.

Write the List Words that rhyme with the pictures.

Write the words that did not rhyme.

Let's Write! On a separate sheet of writing paper, write a recipe for making your favorite flavor of jam. Tell what you best like to eat that has jam on it.

Raft Away

Name _____

Word List

and	am	can	had
dad	cat	bag	man

Unscramble the letters and write the words on the lines.

g a b _____

a n c _____

d a h _____

a t c _____

a d d _____

n a d _____

m a _____

m n a _____

Read each clue. Write the correct word(s) from the Word List.

It begins like _____

It begins like _____

It begins like _____

It begins like _____

It begins like _____

It begins like _____

Let's Write! On a separate sheet of writing paper, write about a special cat.

IF5083 Spelling

Sledding the Slopes

Name _____

Word List

get   let
bed   pen

Word List

fed   hen
web   net

Use the Word List to find and circle each word in the puzzle. Look → .

y	e	b	e	d	h	p	e	n
f	e	d	f	n	g	e	t	d
y	l	e	t	b	w	e	b	m
n	e	t	q	h	e	n	l	p

Write the words you circled.

_____   _____

_____   _____

_____   _____

_____   _____

_____   _____

Circle the misspelled words in each sentence. Then write each sentence correctly on the lines.

1. The hin is in the pin.

_____

_____

2. A bug is in the wab.

_____

_____

3. She fad her cat before med.

_____

_____

4. Lat Fred git the nit.

_____

_____

Let's Write! On a separate sheet of writing paper, write about what you would catch in a net.

Peppy Penguins

Name _____

Word List

best
nest

wet   tent   jet
set   pet   leg

Write the words in ABC order.

1. _____
2. _____
3. _____

4. _____
5. _____
6. _____

7. _____
8. _____

Read each sentence. Write the missing word from the Word List in the boxes.

1. Ned fell and cut his ___ .

2. The hen is in the ___ .

3. Please, ____ the cans in the van.

4. Do you have a _____ rabbit?

5. Ted did his ___ .

6. We will go on a trip in a ____.

7. Dad said, "Yes, you may play in the ____."

8. The hat got _____ when it fell in the pond.

Let's Write! On a separate sheet of writing paper, write about a pet.

 IF5083 Spelling

The Investigating Inspector

Name _____

Word List

in · him · it · fit · big · hid · is · did

Use the Word List to find and circle each hidden word. Then write it on the line.

1. s p f i t m s _____

2. b i s c t e r _____

3. a d i d s a m _____

4. o p i n m t s _____

5. h m i t e n r _____

6. a g n u b i g _____

7. r o m t h i d _____

8. h i m t h r e _____

Read each clue. Write the correct word(s) from the Word List.

1. It begins like (duck) _____

2. It begins like (fan) _____

3. It begins like (bat) _____

4. It begins like (hand) _____

5. It begins like (igloo) _____

This is the HINT

Let's Write! On a separate sheet of writing paper, write about where a pirate hid a treasure.

Picky Pigs

Name _____

Word List

| pig | sit | pin | fin |
| dig | win | hit | lid |

Use the Word List to unscramble the letters on the bibs. Write the word on the line.

t i s _____

t h i _____

p n i _____

i n f _____

i n w _____

g d i _____

g i p _____

i l d _____

Use the Word List to write the missing word in each sentence.

1. She can _____ a pit.

2. Put the _____ on the pan.

3. He will _____ on the bench.

4. Tom _____ the ball into the stands.

5. The _____ sits in the mud.

6. A _____ helps a fish swim.

7. Will he _____ the prize?

8. _____ it on your cap.

Let's Write! On a separate sheet of writing paper, write about a prize you might win.

The Top Poppers

Word List   Name _____

top   nod   dot   box

cot   rod   pop   pot

Write the words in the Word List that rhyme with each picture.

_____   _____
_____   _____
_____   _____

_____   _____
_____   _____

Read the sentences. Write the missing word from the Word List in the boxes.

1. His new fishing _____ came in a _____ .

2. Is it fun to sleep on _____ of a _____ ?

3. This doll can _____ its head up and down.

4. That _____ on the map tells where you live.

5. Use a big _____ to _____ the popcorn.

POPCORN

Let's Write! On a separate sheet of writing paper, write a recipe for making your favorite kind of popcorn treat.

Following the Flock

Name _____

Read each clue. Write the correct word(s) from the Word List.

Word List

It begins like ⬜ _____

It begins like 🐙 _____

It begins like 🚪 _____

It begins like ♪ _____

It begins like ♥ _____

It begins like 🧤 _____

Use the Word List to write the missing word in each sentence. Then draw a line from the sheep to its flock in the same order as your answers.

1. Put it _____ top of the box.

2. Will his _____ let us play?

3. Bob _____ a rock in his sock.

4. That pot is very _____ .

5. A rabbit will _____ on top of the log.

6. We had a _____ of fun at the pond.

7. Rob will _____ up the spilled milk.

8. Ronda did _____ stop at the shop.

rock   box   got   stop   hop   lot   not
on   mom   hot   top   lock   mop   fox

Let's Write! On a separate sheet of writing paper, write about your mom.

Just Tugging Along

Name _____

Word List

bun	jug	rug	tub
up	us	tug	fun

Write the words in the Word List that rhyme with each picture.

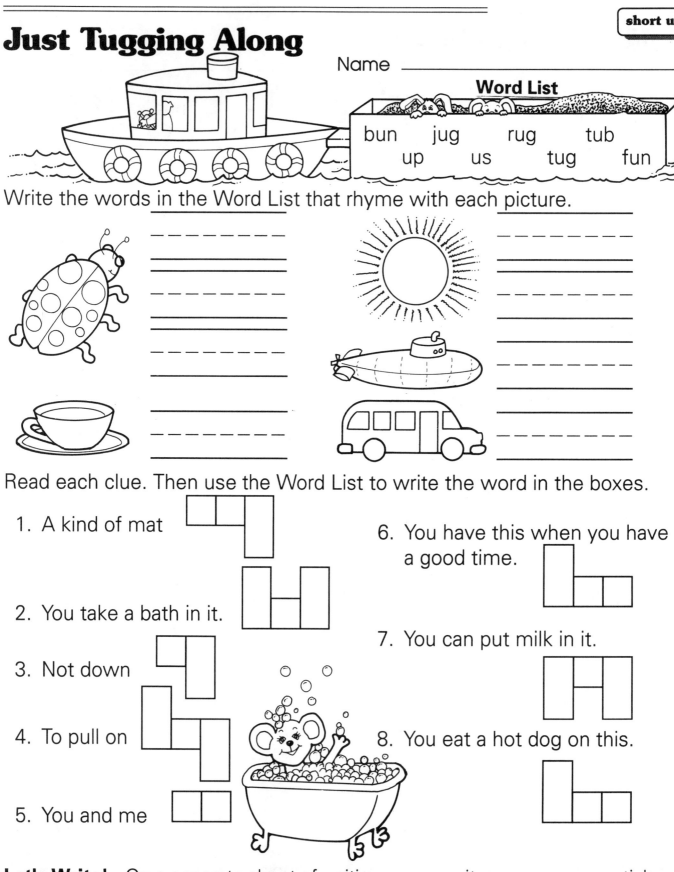

Read each clue. Then use the Word List to write the word in the boxes.

1. A kind of mat

2. You take a bath in it.

3. Not down

4. To pull on

5. You and me

6. You have this when you have a good time.

7. You can put milk in it.

8. You eat a hot dog on this.

Let's Write! On a separate sheet of writing paper, write a newspaper article describing a game of tug-of-war.

Fluttery Butterflies

Word List

Name _____

nut

cup

bug

hug

sun   run

dug   cut

Use the Word List to write the words where they belong.

Nouns or Naming Words		Verbs or Action Words	
_____	_____	_____	_____
_____	_____	_____	_____
_____	_____	_____	_____

Read each sentence. Use the Word List to write the missing word in the boxes.

1. Mom gave me a big _____ for doing my best.

2. I can _____ as fast as Gus.

3. It is hot sitting in the _____ .

4. We _____ a hole for each little plant.

5. Buck put the _____ in the sink.

6. Rusty _____ his hand on the broken glass.

7. The chipmunk grabbed the _____ when it fell from the tree.

8. A red and black _____ ran across my hand.

Let's Write! On a separate sheet of writing paper, write about a butterfly.

Extensions

Short **a** Words (Pages 4 and 5)　　　Name _____

Read the clues. Look at the pictures. Write the words on the lines.

If you can spell **cat**, then you can spell . . .

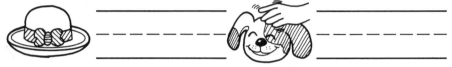 _____　_____　_____

If you can spell **am**, then you can spell . . .

 _____　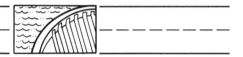 _____　 _____

If you can spell **bag**, then you can spell . . .

 _____　 _____　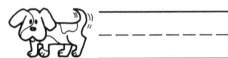 _____

Short **e** Words (Pages 6 and 7)

Read the clues. Write the **short e** words in the puzzle.

Across
1. A color that rhymes with bed
3. More than one man
5. How did you do on the spelling _____ ? (rhymes with best)
6. A doctor for your pets

Down
2. A room in your home that rhymes with ten
3. I _____ the new boy yesterday.
4. You _____ when you take a nap. (rhymes with best)
6. It is something to wear that does not have sleeves. (rhymes with best)

Short **i** Words (Pages 8 and 9)

Read the clues. Write the words on the lines.

It begins like [spiderweb] and rhymes with [pig]. _____

It begins like [kite] and rhymes with [lid]. _____

It begins like [bell] and rhymes with [bench]. _____

It begins like [boot] and rhymes with [pin]. _____

Short **o** Words (Pages 10 and 11)

Write the name of each picture on the lines. Then change the letter in the circle to the one shown. Write the new word on the line.

[box] ( )_____ change the circled letter to **f** _____

[mop] ( )_____ change the circled letter to **c** _____

[top] ___( )___ change the circled letter to **t** _____

[pot] ( )_____ change the circled letter to **j** _____

[cot] ___( )___ change the circled letter to **b** _____

Short **u** Words (Pages 12 and 13)

Write the name of each picture.

[igloo] _____ [submarine] _____ [dog] _____

[bear] _____ [gum] _____ [bus] _____

Tasty Cakes

Word List   Name _____

made
take

name
game

came
gave

bake
gate

Say the name of each picture. Use the Word List to write the words that rhyme with it.

Write the two words in the Word List that you did not use.

Write the letter that is at the end of every word. _____

Use the Word List to complete the puzzle.

Across

2. Would you like to play a _____ ?
3. His dog _____ when he called him.
5. Lock the _____ when you go.
7. Can you _____ a cake?

Down

1. What is your last _____ ?
2. He _____ his sister a gift.
4. We _____ a tent with blankets.
6. Please _____ your coat with you.

Let's Write! On a separate sheet of writing paper, write a recipe for your favorite kind of cake.

Hey! It's Raining!

Name _____

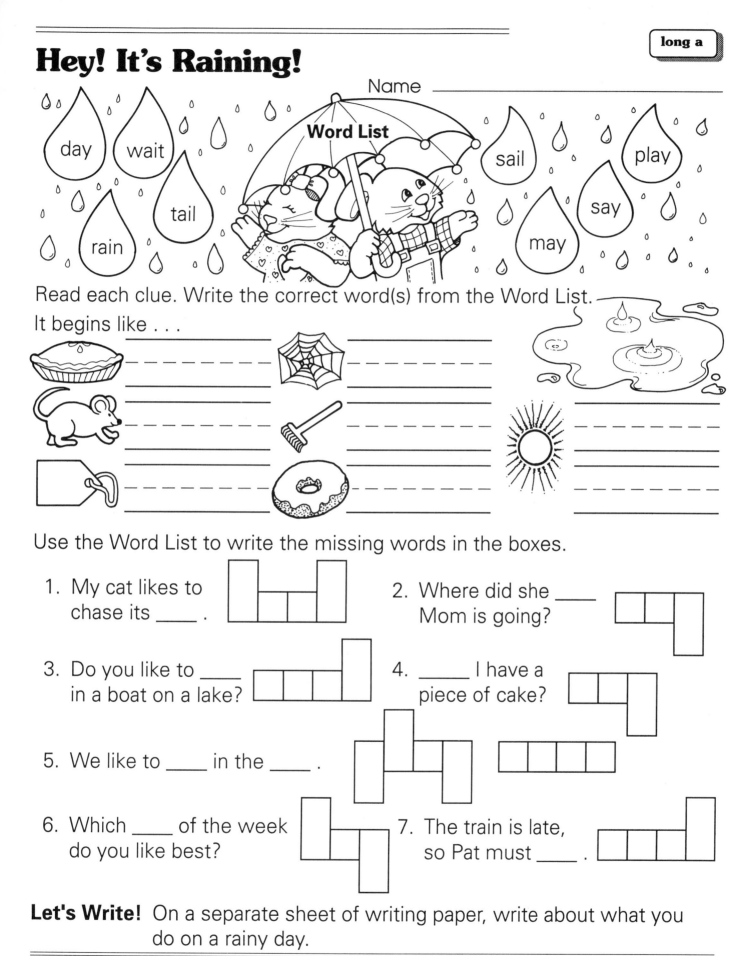

Word List

day · wait · tail · rain · sail · play · say · may

Read each clue. Write the correct word(s) from the Word List.

It begins like . . .

Use the Word List to write the missing words in the boxes.

1. My cat likes to chase its ____ .

2. Where did she ____ Mom is going?

3. Do you like to ____ in a boat on a lake?

4. ____ I have a piece of cake?

5. We like to ____ in the ____ .

6. Which ____ of the week do you like best?

7. The train is late, so Pat must ____ .

Let's Write! On a separate sheet of writing paper, write about what you do on a rainy day.

Sneak a Peek!

Name _____

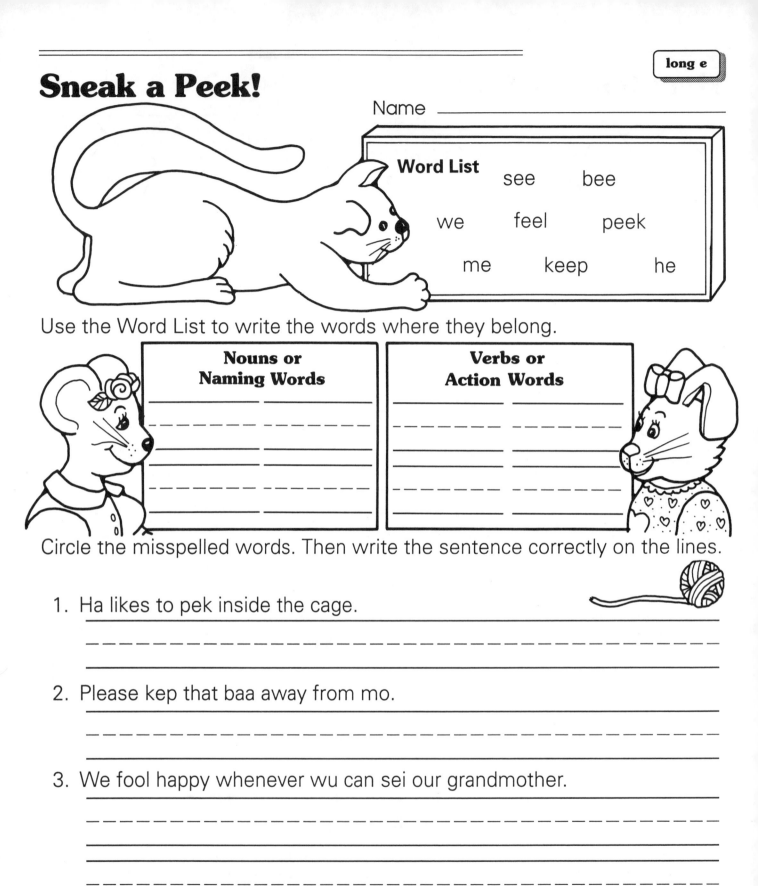

Word List

	see	bee
we	feel	peek
me	keep	he

Use the Word List to write the words where they belong.

Nouns or Naming Words	Verbs or Action Words

Circle the misspelled words. Then write the sentence correctly on the lines.

1. Ha likes to pek inside the cage.

_____

_____

2. Please kep that baa away from mo.

_____

_____

3. We fool happy whenever wu can sei our grandmother.

_____

_____

_____

Let's Write! On a separate sheet of writing paper, write about what a cat found when it sneaked a peek inside a paper bag.

Tea Time

Name _____

Word List

eat read sea seal leaf leap neat lead

Use the Word List to unscramble the letters on each tea bag. Write the words correctly on the lines.

aple _____ esla _____ tea _____

dale _____ esa _____ afle _____

etna _____ erda _____

Which two letters are the same in every word? _____

Read each sentence. Use the Word List to find the missing word. Write the word in the boxes.

1. The _____ dived into the _____ .

2. The little plant has one green _____ .

3. Did you _____ the new book in the library?

4. Can you _____ over that mud puddle?

5. Steve can _____ the class to the bus.

6. Megan keeps her desk very _____ .

7. What did you _____ for lunch today?

Let's Write! On a separate sheet of writing paper, write about a new flavor of tea.

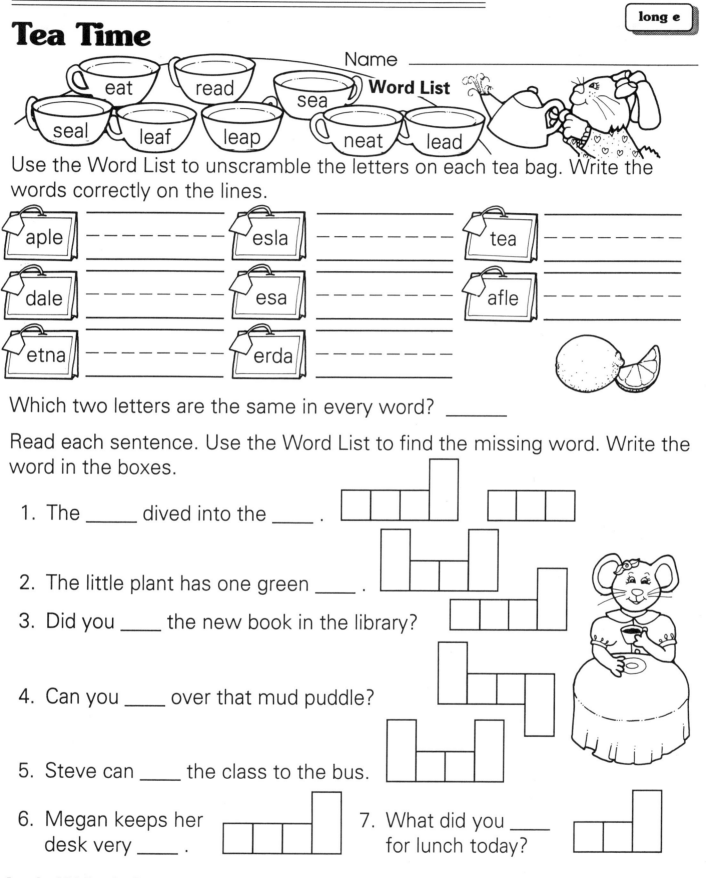

In the "Lime" Light

Name _____

Word List

line, tie, dive, bite, side, hide, l, wipe

Write the words in ABC order.

1. _____   4. _____   7. _____

2. _____   5. _____   8. _____

3. _____   6. _____

Use the Word List to complete the puzzle.

Across

3. The kitten likes to ____ under the bed.
4. Put the book on the left ____ of your desk.
7. Please ____ up the spilled milk.

Down

1. There was a long ____ at the bank.
2. Did the puppy ____ the slipper?
5. The seals will ____ off the rocks.
6. Can you ____ a ribbon on the gift?

Which word on the list was not used in the puzzle? _____

Let's Write! On a separate sheet of writing paper, write what you would say to a news reporter if you had just won an Olympic medal for diving.

A Miner's Find

Name _____

like	time	ride	fine
size	mine	tide	hike

Say the name of each picture. Use the Word List to write the word(s) that rhymes with it.

_____

_____

Write the word from the Word List that did not rhyme. _____

Use the Word List to write the missing word in the boxes.

1. That gray and white cat is _____ .

2. Mike will _____ his bike to school.

3. What _____ box do you need for the gift?

4. It is a _____ day to take a _____ .

5. Do you _____ to eat pizza?

6. At what _____ does the _____ roll in?

Let's Write! On a separate sheet of writing paper, write about finding an old mine while you and a friend are on a hike.

Noticeable Notes

home	hope

Name _____

Word List

go	hole	so	note	rope	no

Read each clue. Write the correct word(s) from the Word List.

It begins like . . .

_____

_____

_____

_____

_____

_____

Use the Word List to write the missing words in the boxes.

1. May we _____ to the store later?

2. Robin wrote a _____ to his dad.

3. It is _____ cold that there is ice on the street.

4. We _____ that we can go on a trip.

5. They will go _____ after the football game.

6. There is _____ other road to the coast.

7. The workmen dropped the ___ into the ___ .

Let's Write! On a separate sheet of writing paper, write a short note to your mom, dad, teacher, or friend.

Toads on the Go!

Name _____

Word List

soap · road · loaf · boat · coat · goat · toast · oats

Match each picture with a sentence. Write the missing word on the line.

1. Flo the toad is putting on a _____ .

2. Mort the toad hops down the _____ .

3. Norton the toad butters the _____ .

4. Cody the toad rows a _____ .

5. One toad takes a bath with lots of _____ .

6. Rosey the toad sits on a brown _____ .

7. Sophie the toad is eating some _____ .

8. Dory the toad baked a _____ of bread.

One toad did not have a name. Give the toad a name that has the

long o sound in it. _____

Let's Write! On a separate sheet of writing paper, write about a toad that leaves home to explore the world.

Extensions

Name _____

Long a Words (Pages 16 and 17)

Read the clues. Look at the pictures. Write the words on the lines.

If you can spell **take**, then
you can spell . . .

_____

If you can spell **gave**, then
you can spell . . .

_____

If you can spell **may**, then
you can spell . . .

THIS ➡

_____

If you can spell **nail**, then
you can spell . . .

_____

Long e Words (Pages 18 and 19)

Write the word that names this picture. Circle
the two letters that make the **long e** sound.

_____

Read each sentence. Use the two letters you circled above to write the
missing words in the boxes.

1. She broke the ____ of her shoe.

2. The water in the pond
   is very ____ .

3. We will go on a
   trip next ____ .

Write the word that names this picture. Circle
the two letters that make the **long e** sound.

_____

Read each sentence. Use the two letters you circled above to write the
missing words in the boxes.

1. That bird has a very
   big ____.

2. It is not nice to be
   ____ to anyone.

3. Pete plays on the
   baseball ____ .

Long **i** Words (Pages 20 and 21)

Write the word that names this picture. Circle the letter that makes the **long i** sound.

Read each clue. Use the letter you circled above to write the words in the puzzle.

Across

3. Do you like to fly a ____ ?
5. The ____ cone fell from the tree.
6. The number before ten is ____ .
7. A ____ is worth 10 cents.

Down

1. The bees made a ____ .
2. This red apple is very ____ .
4. The number after four is ___ .

Long **o** Words (Pages 22 and 23)

Write the word that names this picture. Circle the letter that makes the **long o** sound.

Use the letter you circled above to write the name of each picture.

Write the word that names this picture. Circle the two letters that make the **long o** sound.

Use the letters you circled above to write the name of each picture.

Cracker Crunchers

Word List

free · prize · drive · frog · cross · grass · train · grade

Name _____

Look at each clue. Write the correct word(s) from the Word List. It begins like . . .

Circle the misspelled words. Then write the words correctly on the lines.

1. Look both ways before you kros the street.

2. My sister is in the first jraid.

3. A butterfly landed on the blade of graz.

4. She gave us a fee pass to the baseball game.

5. A little froj jumped into the pond.

6. They rode the little chrain around the zoo.

7. Gus won the grand prise in the spelling contest.

8. His mother will div them to school.

Let's Write: On a separate sheet of writing paper, write about a new, super-crunchy cracker.

Fluffy Flapjacks

Name _____

Word List
plus, float, place, plane, fly, glide, clap, flat

Use the Word List to unscramble the letters on each flapjack. Write the words correctly in the boxes.

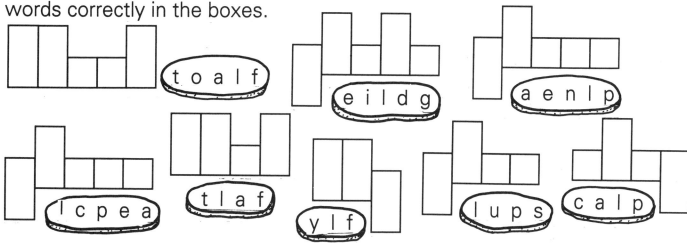

t o a l f
e i l d g
a e n l p
l c p e a
t l a f
y l f
l u p s
c a l p

Use the Word List to write the missing words on the lines.

1. Two ____ ____ ____ ____ two will equal four.

2. A toy boat will ____ ____ ____ ____ ____ in the pond.

3. Glen's bike has a ____ ____ ____ ____ tire.

4. The little bird cannot ____ ____ ____ yet.

5. Our new sled will ____ ____ ____ ____ ____ down the hill.

6. They waited for the ____ ____ ____ ____ ____ to land.

7. We can ____ ____ ____ ____ along while they sing the song.

8. This is the best ____ ____ ____ ____ ____ to eat tacos.

Let's Write! On a separate sheet of writing paper, write about the fluffiest flapjack in the world.

Spill Spongers

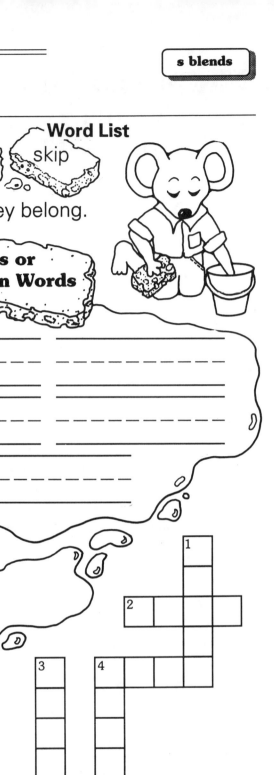

snap sled smell snail
stove spin sleep skip

Name _____

Word List

Use the Word List to write the words where they belong.

Nouns or Naming Words

_____
_____
_____
_____
_____

Verbs or Action Words

_____ _____
_____ _____
_____ _____
_____ _____
_____

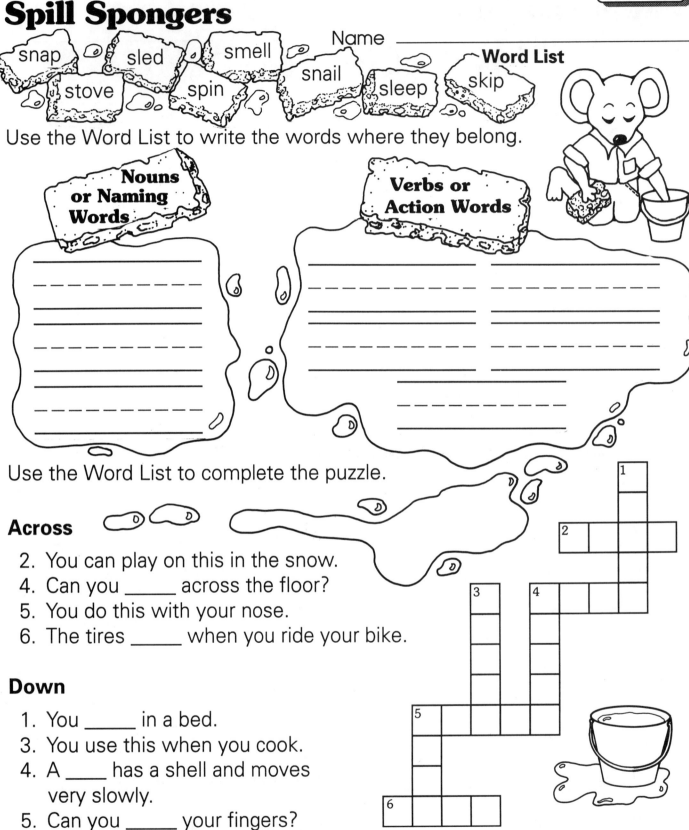

Use the Word List to complete the puzzle.

Across

2. You can play on this in the snow.
4. Can you _____ across the floor?
5. You do this with your nose.
6. The tires _____ when you ride your bike.

Down

1. You _____ in a bed.
3. You use this when you cook.
4. A _____ has a shell and moves very slowly.
5. Can you _____ your fingers?

Let's Write! On a separate sheet of writing paper, write a poem about using a sponge to wipe up a spill.

Cheer Up!

Name _____

Word List

chop   check   chain   child

chin   cheek   children   chase

Say the name of each picture. Use the Word List to write the word(s) that rhymes with it.

Which words did not rhyme with any of the pictures?

Read the sentences. Use the Word List to complete the puzzle.

Across

3. They will use a _____ to pull the car.
5. Many _____ like to go to the circus.
6. Write a _____ mark in the correct box.

Down

1. The baby spilled food on his _____ .
2. Only one _____ is on the slide.
4. They like to run and _____ each other.
6. Dad will _____ the stump into logs.
7. The kitten licked the girl's _____ .

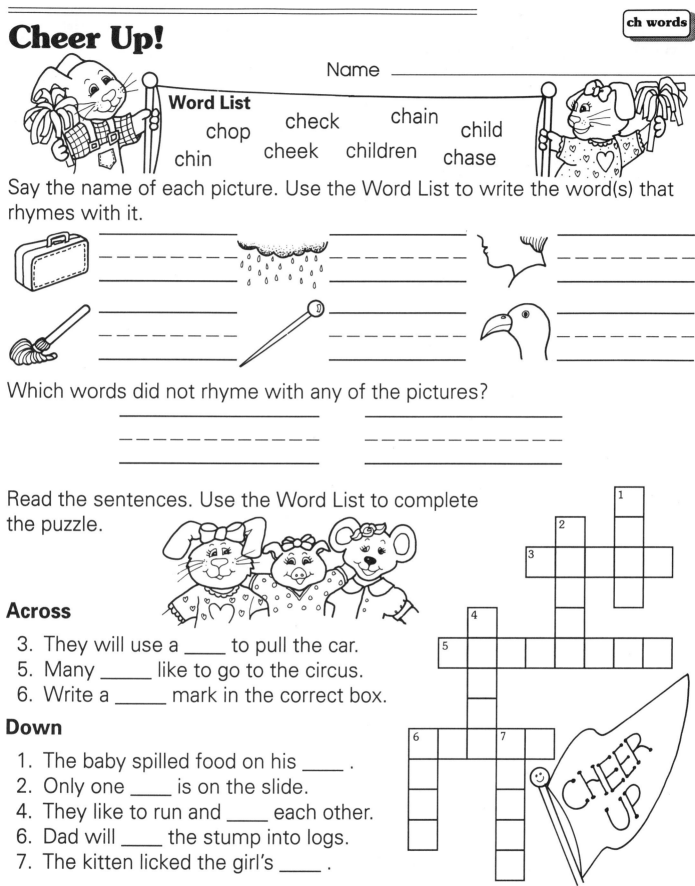

Let's Write! On a separate sheet of writing paper, write a "cheer" for your class.

Shuttling Around

Word List shake shape sheep shop shell shut ship she

Name _____

Use the Word List to write the words in which you hear the same vowel sound as in the picture.

_____

_____

_____

_____

_____

_____

_____

_____

_____

Use the Word List to write the missing word on the lines.

1. A flock of _____ graze on the hillside.

2. The _____ will sail from the dock very soon.

3. We must keep the gate _____ to keep the dog in.

4. Please _____ the bottle of salad dressing.

5. A square is a _____ that has four equal sides.

6. Do you like to _____ at the mall?

7. Do you think that _____ will come to visit us?

8. The clam always stays inside its _____ .

Let's Write! On a separate sheet of writing paper, write about traveling as an astronaut in a space shuttle.

Whistle a Tune

Word List

which whip whale why where when what wheel

Name _____

Use the Word List to write the words that ask questions in the boxes.

Use the Word List to find the words that
name things. Write them in the boxes.

Read each sentence. Use the Word List to write the missing words.

1. _____ are we going this afternoon?

2. _____ red dress will Wendy buy?

3. A huge _____ swam near the shore.

4. _____ are they going to the basketball game?

5. The shopping cart has a broken _____ .

6. _____ will we see at the zoo?

7. Leon sat down when his trainer snapped the _____ .

8. _____ is Mother Duck taking her ducklings to the pond?

Let's Write! On a separate sheet of writing paper, write a poem about
whistles or whistling.

Thundering, Thumping Clouds

Word List

those
there that this
them the then they

Name _____

Use the Word List to find and circle the words in the puzzle.
Look → and ↓.

t	t	d	t	t	t	t	h	e
h	h	o	h	h	h	e	t	h
e	e	y	i	e	o	s	h	e
m	y	e	s	r	s	d	e	s
t	h	a	t	e	e	t	n	o

Write the words you circled.

_____ _____
_____ _____
_____ _____
_____ _____
_____ _____

Read each sentence. Use the Word List to write the missing words in the boxes.

1. Is _____ your coat on _____ last hook?

2. Are _____ coming to pick you up after school?

3. Do _____ books over there belong to you?

4. We will have a picnic, _____ we will go on a hike.

5. _____ are two slices of pizza left for _____ .

6. Please take _____ apple to your teacher.

Let's Write!   On a separate sheet of writing paper, write about a thunderstorm or about what it would be like if you were a thundercloud.

32

Extensions

r Blend Words (Page 26)

Read the words. Circle the two letters that form the **r** blend in each word.

grain   friend   treat   cream

Use the Word List to write the missing words on the lines.

_____

1. My _____ and I like to hike trails.

2. Tracy likes whipped _____ on her pudding.

3. It is important that you _____ others kindly.

4. It is time for the farmer to harvest the _____ .

l Blend Words (Page 27)

Match each group of letters to a blend. Write the words on the lines.

ad   ub   ant   iff   ag   obe   ug   ake

pl	**fl**	**gl**	**cl**
_____	_____	_____	_____
_____	_____	_____	_____
_____	_____	_____	_____
_____	_____	_____	_____

s Blend Words (Page 28)

Match each **s** blend to a group of letters to make a word. One is done for you.

st	ile	<u>stop</u>	sn	eed	_____
sm	ace	_____	sl	eeze	_____
sp	op	_____	sp	ide	_____

ch and **sh** Words (Pages 29 and 30)

Read the words.

chick
shed

shark
champ

chime
shine

shave
chair

Write the words that make the sound you hear at the beginning of 🐑 .

_____   _____   _____   _____

_____   _____   _____   _____

Write the words that make the sound you hear at the beginning of √ .

_____   _____   _____   _____

_____   _____   _____   _____

wh and **th** Words (Pages 31 and 32)

Match each group of letters to the **th** or **wh** letters.
Write the words
on the lines.

orn   ick   ank   ile

iskers   eat   isper   ink

w h   **t h**

_____   _____

_____   _____

_____   _____

_____   _____

_____   _____

Naturally Colorful Canvas

Name _____

Use the code in the Word List to color the picture.

Word List

1–brown	6–green
2–white	7–yellow
3–blue	8–red
4–black	9–orange
5–pink	10–purple

Use the picture to write the missing color words on the lines.

The _____ cub is eating a _____ berry. A _____

caterpillar is creeping under a _____ flower. One _____

duck and one _____ fish are swimming in the _____

pond. A little _____ bird is resting on a rock. A _____

butterfly will land on the _____ flower.

Let's Write! On a separate sheet of paper, draw and color a picture. Then write sentences to describe what is happening in your picture.

Now, on the Count of . . .

Name _____

Word List

one   two

three   four   five

six   seven   eight

nine   ten

Trace each number and write its number word next to it.

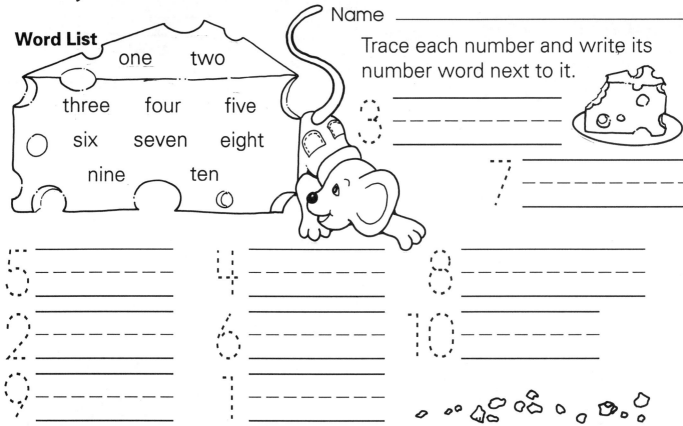

3 _____

7 _____

5 _____

4 _____

8 _____

2 _____

6 _____

10 _____

9 _____

1 _____

Work the problems. Write the answers on the lines. Then write the answers using the correct number words in the puzzle.

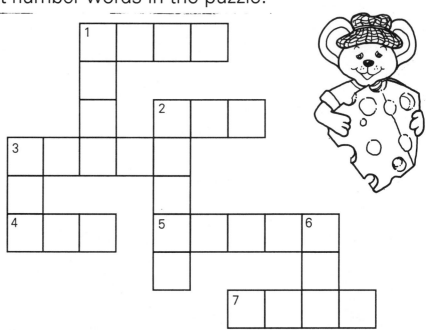

Across
1. 3 + 2 = ____
2. 4 + 2 = ____
3. 2 + 1 = ____
4. 1 + 0 = ____
5. 5 + 3 = ____
7. 2 + 7 = ____

Down
1. 2 + 2 = ____
2. 4 + 3 = ____
3. 0 + 2 = ____
6. 4 + 6 = ____

Let's Write! On a separate sheet of writing paper, write a math problem using three or more number words.

Correctly Positioned

Name _____

Word List   after   last

right   before   <u>first</u>

left   now   next

Read the sentences. Use the Word List to write the missing word in the boxes.

1. Buck will read the ____ story.

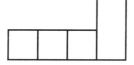

2. We must go to the bus stop ____ .

3. We must get some logs ____ we can build a fire.

4. That is the ____ slice of pizza.

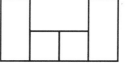

5. Plant the flowers to the ____ of the tree.

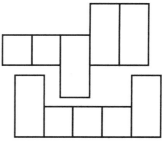

6. This is the ____ time she will sing by herself.

7. Go to the ____, not the right.

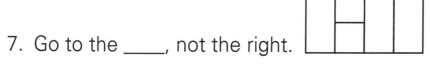

8. She will go to bed ____ she brushes her teeth.

Let's Write! Imagine that you are a sportswriter for a newspaper. On a separate sheet of writing paper, write about a great baseball game.

It's in Sight!

Name _____

Word List are   to   you   of

said   was   goes   have

Write the words in ABC order.

1. _____   4. _____   7. _____

2. _____   5. _____   8. _____

3. _____   6. _____

Write the missing words on the lines. Use the numbered letters to solve the code.

1. The class will be at the farm most ___ ___ the day.
   $\underset{1}{\qquad}$

2. Andy and Amy ___ ___ ___ ___ three kittens.
   $\underset{2}{\qquad} \quad \underset{3}{\qquad}$

3. Grandmother sent a letter ___ ___ Shane.
   $\underset{4}{\qquad}$

4. Jan and Donna ___ ___ ___ going to the horse show.
   $\underset{5}{\qquad}$

5. Sam ___ ___ ___ ___ that he can play the drums.
   $\underset{6}{\qquad} \underset{7}{\qquad}$

6. She ___ ___ ___ ___ to the lake every summer.
   $\underset{8}{\qquad}$

7. Do ___ ___ ___ like to go camping in the forest?
   $\underset{9}{\qquad} \quad \underset{10}{\qquad}$

8. The puppy ___ ___ ___ asleep in the basket.
   $\underset{11}{\qquad}$

___ ___ ___ ___ ___ !   ___ ___ ___   ___ ___ ___
8 5 3 11 4   9 1 10   7 6 7

___ ___   ___ ___ ___ ___ ___ !
6 4   5 6 8 2 4

Let's Write! On a separate sheet of writing paper, write about the most beautiful sight you have ever seen.

Take Note of These Words

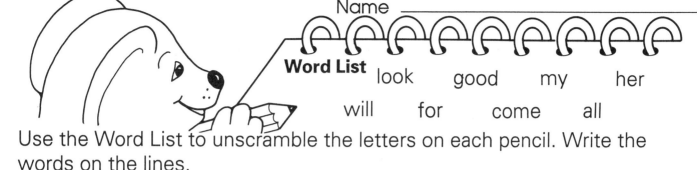

Name _____

Word List   look   good   my   her
will   for   come   all

Use the Word List to unscramble the letters on each pencil. Write the words on the lines.

r h e → _ _ _ _ _ _ _

d o g o → _ _ _ _ _ _ _

r o f → _ _ _ _ _ _ _

l o k o → _ _ _ _ _ _ _

y m → _ _ _ _ _ _ _

o m c e → _ _ _ _ _ _ _

l a l → _ _ _ _ _ _ _

l i l w → _ _ _ _ _ _ _

Use the Word List to write the missing word on the lines.

1. Did you have a ___ ___ ___ ___ time at the party?

2. They ___ ___ ___ ___ help rake the grass.

3. Ted and Jack will ___ ___ ___ ___ here later.

4. Amy is happy that ___ ___ ___ grandmother is coming to visit.

5. Did you remember to ___ ___ ___ ___ for your lost coat?

6. Will ___ ___ ___ of those boxes fit in the car?

7. This letter is ___ ___ ___ you.

8. Those are ___ ___ glasses on the desk.

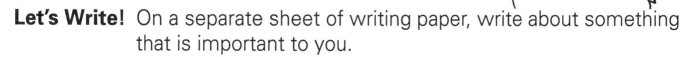

Let's Write! On a separate sheet of writing paper, write about something that is important to you.

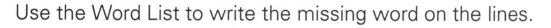

Don't Get Lost!

Name _____

Use the Word List to unscramble the letters on each backpack. Write the words correctly in the boxes.

o b g l e

u t s h o

a p m

e s w t

o r t n h

s t a e

d a n l

r w t a e

Use the Word List to help you label the pictures.

Let's Write! On a separate sheet of paper, draw a map that shows how to go from one place to another. Then tell how to follow the map.

Review

Color Words (Page 35)

Name _____

Read each sentence. Write the correct color word on the lines.

1. A strawberry milkshake is _____ .

2. Your shadow is _____ . 3. A stoplight is _____ .

4. A polar bear is _____ . 5. Cucumbers are _____ .

6. Some tree branches are _____ .

7. Water in a swimming pool often looks _____ .

8. Grapes can be white, red, green, or _____ .

9. A ripe pumpkin is _____ .

10. A nugget of gold is _____ .

Number Words (Page 36)

Count the number of berries on each bush. Write the correct number word on the lines.

 _____  _____  _____

 _____  _____  _____

 _____  _____

Review

Name _____

Position Words (Page 37)

Look at the picture. Read each sentence. Unscramble the letters at the end of the sentence to correctly spell the missing word.

The clown is the _____ one in the parade. (i s f r t)

The elephant is _____ . (e n x t)

The elephant is _____ the monkey. (e o b r f e)

The bear is _____ the monkey. (t r a f e)

The monkey is to the _____ of the bear. (e l f t)

The elephant is to the _____ of the clown. (r g i h t)

The bear is the _____ one in the parade. (t s a l)

Frequently Misspelled Words (Pages 38 and 39)

Circle the missing word that is spelled correctly and write it on the line.

1. You _____ find the slipper if you _____ under the bed.
   wil   will   look   luk

2. It is a _____ day for the class picnic.
   gud   good

3. Jack is _____ best friend. 4. The bus will _____ soon.
   mi   my   kome   come

5. Donna likes to play catch with _____ brother.
   her   hur   _____

6. We will _____ ride in the same car.   – – – – – – – –
   oll   all   _____

Geographic Terms (Page 40)

Label the directions on the compass rose.

Fun Spelling Activities

Vary the practice of the weekly word lists by using one of these activities. You will find these activities appropriate for individual, paired, or cooperative group use.

- One student reads the words from the Word List as the other(s) . . .
  —writes the words on a small individual chalkboard.
  —types the words on a typewriter or computer.
  —spells the words aloud.
  —spells the words aloud into a tape recorder.
  —uses individual letter cards to spell the words.
  —uses individual rubber, plastic, or wooded letters to spell the words.

- One student selects a word from the list and places individual plastic letters or letter cards in a scrambled order. Another student then arranges the letters to spell the word correctly.

- One student gives the definition of a word as the other(s) spells it aloud or writes it.

- Cut square blocks from 3" Styrofoam™. Write the spelling words for the week on masking tape. Tape a different word to each side of the block. One student rolls the block and reads the word that shows on top. The other student(s) spells it.

- When appropriate, have the students use magazines, newspaper inserts, and catalogs to find and cut out pictures that illustrate the words on the Word List. Paste the pictures to a sheet of paper and label each picture with the correct word.

- Students draw pictures to illustrate the words on the Word List and write sentences about their pictures.

- Create word sorts according to similar elements.

- Give each student a large triangular piece of brightly colored butcher paper on which to write the week's word list twice—once on each side. They may decorate the banner after writing the words.

- Give the students sentence strips or large index cards on which to write each of the spelling words. After writing the words, they then use glue to trace over each word. When dry, they will be able to feel the raised letters as they trace over the word with their fingers, thus giving them a tactile sense for studying the words.

- Give the students strips of butcher paper, tagboard, or large index cards. Students then "spell" the words by gluing pieces of macaroni, rice, cereal pieces, etc. in the shape of the letters. For some students, you may want to have them write the words first and then glue the media to the letters.

- Give each student a stick of clay to roll out into a medium-sized square or circle. As the teacher/ student says a list word, the student(s) uses a pencil or toothpick to "etch" or write the word in the clay. Smooth over the clay between words.

- Practice writing the words using assorted materials.
  —lengths of string or yarn
  —pipe cleaners bent to form the letters
  —colorful markers
  —crayons

- Set up an easel and have the student "paint" (write) the Word List.

- Have students do fingerpainting with the Word List.

- Give the students a sheet of grid paper to make their own Wordsearch Puzzles.

- Students create their own crossword puzzles for the words on the Word List. When completed, the students exchange papers and have fun working each other's puzzles.

- Have the students make their own dictionaries in which to write the spelling list words and their own "special" list of words. Staple 26 sheets of writing paper together along the left edge or the top. Have the students write one letter, capital and lowercase, at the top of each page. This is to be used throughout the school year.

Answer Key
Spelling
Grade 1

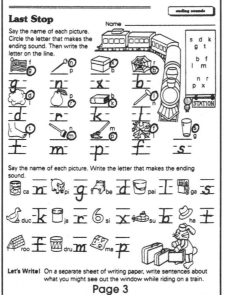

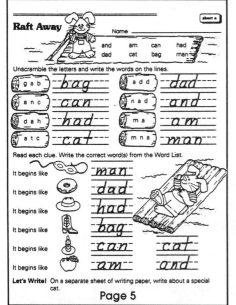

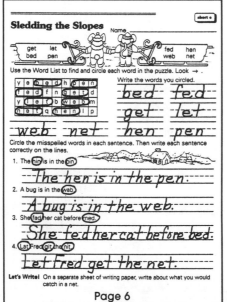

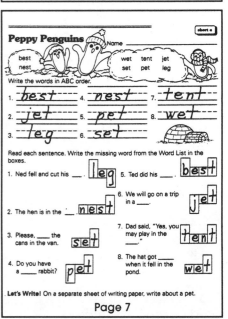

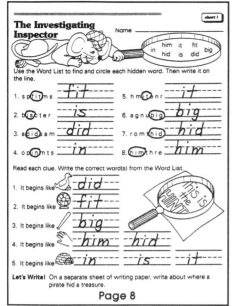

The Investigating Inspector

short i

Name _____

Word List: him it fit / in hid is did big

Use the Word List to find and circle each hidden word. Then write it on the line.

1. s p x i t m s — *fit*
2. b x s t e r — *is*
3. a d i d s a m — *did*
4. o p i n t s — *in*
5. h m i t e n r — *it*
6. a g n u b i g — *big*
7. r o m h i d — *hid*
8. h i m t h r e — *him*

Read each clue. Write the correct word(s) from the Word List.

1. It begins like 🦆 — *did*
2. It begins like 🐟 — *fit*
3. It begins like 🕯 — *big*
4. It begins like ✋ — *him* *hid*
5. It begins like 🏠 — *in* *is* *it*

Let's Write! On a separate sheet of writing paper, write about where a pirate hid a treasure.

Page 8

Picky Pigs

short i

Name _____

Word List: pig sit pin fin / dig win hit lid

Use the Word List to unscramble the letters on the bibs. Write the word on the line.

sit *hit* *pin*
fin *win* *dig*
pig *lid*

Use the Word List to write the missing word in each sentence.

1. She can *dig* a pit.
2. Put the *lid* on the pan.
3. He will *sit* on the bench.
4. Tom *hit* the ball into the stands.
5. The *pig* sits in the mud.
6. A *fin* helps a fish swim.
7. Will he *win* the prize?
8. *Pin* it on your cap.

Let's Write! On a separate sheet of writing paper, write about a prize you might win.

Page 9

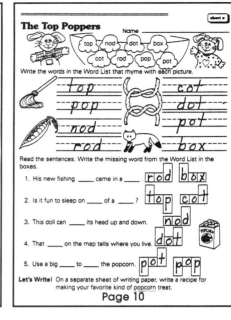

The Top Poppers

short o

Name _____

Word List: top nod dot box / cot rod pop pot

Write the words in the Word List that rhyme with each picture.

top *cot*
pop *dot*
nod *pot*
rod *box*

Read the sentences. Write the missing word from the Word List in the boxes.

1. His new fishing ___ came in a ___. — *rod* *box*
2. Is it fun to sleep on ___ of a ___? — *top* *cot*
3. This doll can ___ its head up and down. — *nod*
4. That ___ on the map tells where you live. — *dot*
5. Use a big ___ to ___ the popcorn. — *pot* *pop*

Let's Write! On a separate sheet of writing paper, write a recipe for making your favorite kind of popcorn treat.

Page 10

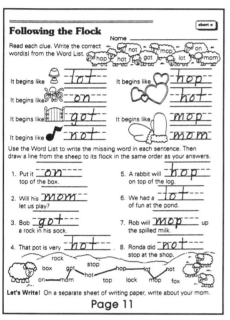

Following the Flock

short o

Name _____

Word List: not mop on / hop hot got lot mom

Read each clue. Write the correct word(s) from the Word List.

It begins like — *lot*
It begins like — *on*
It begins like — *got*
It begins like 🎵 — *not*

It begins like — *hop*
It begins like ❤️ — *hot*
It begins like 🧤 — *mop*
— *mom*

Use the Word List to write the missing word in each sentence. Then draw a line from the sheep to its flock in the same order as your answers.

1. Put it *on* top of the box.
2. Will his *mom* let us play?
3. Bob *got* a rock in his sock.
4. That pot is very *hot*.
5. A rabbit will *hop* on top of the log.
6. We had a *lot* of fun at the pond.
7. Rob will *mop* up the spilled milk.
8. Ronda did *not* stop at the shop.

rock box got hot hop lot not
on mom top lock mop fox

Let's Write! On a separate sheet of writing paper, write about your mom.

Page 11

Just Tugging Along

short u

Name _____

Word List: bun jug rug tub / up us tug fun

Write the words in the Word List that rhyme with each picture.

tug *bun*
rug *fun*
jug *tub*
up *us*

Read each clue. Then use the Word List to write the word in the boxes.

1. A kind of mat — *rug*
2. You take a bath in it. — *tub*
3. Not down — *up*
4. To pull on — *tug*
5. You and me — *us*
6. You have this when you have a good time. — *fun*
7. You can put milk in it. — *jug*
8. You eat a hot dog on this. — *bun*

Let's Write! On a separate sheet of writing paper, write a newspaper article describing a game of tug-of-war.

Page 12

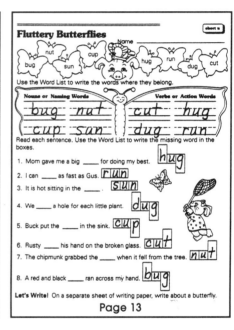

Fluttery Butterflies

short u

Name _____

Word List: nut cup / bug sun hug run dug cut

Use the Word List to write the words where they belong.

Nouns or Naming Words		Verbs or Action Words	
bug	*nut*	*cut*	*hug*
cup	*sun*	*dug*	*run*

Read each sentence. Use the Word List to write the missing word in the boxes.

1. Mom gave me a big ___ for doing my best. — *hug*
2. I can ___ as fast as Gus. — *run*
3. It is hot sitting in the ___. — *sun*
4. We ___ a hole for each little plant. — *dug*
5. Buck put the ___ in the sink. — *cup*
6. Rusty ___ his hand on the broken glass. — *cut*
7. The chipmunk grabbed the ___ when it fell from the tree. — *nut*
8. A red and black ___ ran across my hand. — *bug*

Let's Write! On a separate sheet of writing paper, write about a butterfly.

Page 13

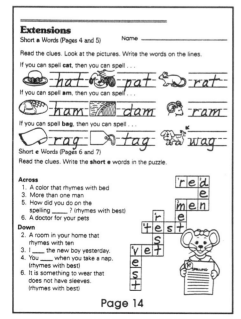

Extensions

Short a Words (Pages 4 and 5)

Name _____

Read the clues. Look at the pictures. Write the words on the lines.

If you can spell **cat**, then you can spell . . .
hat *pat* *rat*

If you can spell **am**, then you can spell . . .
ham *dam* *ram*

If you can spell **bag**, then you can spell . . .
rag *tag* *wag*

Short e Words (Pages 6 and 7)
Read the clues. Write the **short e** words in the puzzle.

Across
1. A color that rhymes with bed
3. More than one man
5. How did you do on the spelling ___ ? (rhymes with best)
6. A doctor for your pets

Down
2. A room in your home that rhymes with ten
3. I ___ the new boy yesterday.
4. You ___ when you take a nap. (rhymes with best)
6. It is something to wear that does not have sleeves. (rhymes with best)

red
men
test
vest

Page 14

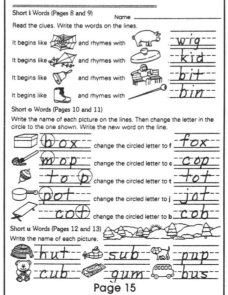

Short i Words (Pages 8 and 9)

Name _____

Read the clues. Write the words on the lines.

It begins like 🕸 and rhymes with 🐷 — *wig*
It begins like 🪁 and rhymes with — *kid*
It begins like 🔔 and rhymes with — *bit*
It begins like 👢 and rhymes with — *bin*

Short o Words (Pages 10 and 11)
Write the name of each picture on the lines. Then change the letter in the circle to the one shown. Write the new word on the line.

box change the circled letter to f — *fox*
mop change the circled letter to c — *cop*
top change the circled letter to t — *tot*
pot change the circled letter to j — *jot*
cot change the circled letter to b — *cob*

Short u Words (Pages 12 and 13)
Write the name of each picture.

hut *sub* *pup*
cub *gum* *bus*

Page 15

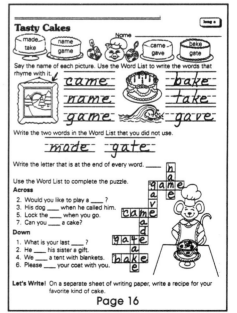

Tasty Cakes

long a

Name _____

Word List: made take name game / came gave bake gate

Say the name of each picture. Use the Word List to write the words that rhyme with it.

came *bake*
name *take*
game *gave*

Write the two words in the Word List that you did not use.
made *gate*

Write the letter that is at the end of every word. ___

Use the Word List to complete the puzzle.

Across
2. Would you like to play a ___ ?
3. His dog ___ when he called him.
5. Lock the ___ when you go.
7. Can you ___ a cake?

Down
1. What is your last ___ ?
2. He ___ his sister a gift.
4. We ___ a tent with blankets.
6. Please ___ your coat with you.

name game came made gate bake

Let's Write! On a separate sheet of writing paper, write a recipe for your favorite kind of cake.

Page 16

Hey! It's Raining!
long a

Name _____

day   wait   sail   play   tail   rain   say   may

Read each clue. Write the correct word(s) from the Word List. It begins like . . .

play   wait   may   rain   say   tail   day   sail

Use the Word List to write the missing words in the boxes.

1. My cat likes to chase its ___   tail
2. Where did she ___ Mom is going?   say
3. Do you like to ___ in a boat on a lake?   sail
4. I have a piece of cake!   May
5. We like to ___ in the ___.   play   rain
6. Which ___ of the week do you like best?   day
7. The train is late, so Pat must ___   wait

Let's Write! On a separate sheet of writing paper, write about what you do on a rainy day.

Page 17

Sneak a Peek!
long e

Name _____

he   see   bee   we   feel   peek   me   keep

Use the Word List to write the words where they belong.

Nouns or Naming Words		Verbs or Action Words	
we	me	feel	see
bee	he	keep	peek

Circle the misspelled words. Then write the sentence correctly on the lines.

1. He likes to peek inside the cage.

   He likes to peek inside the cage.

2. Please keep that bee away from me.

   Please keep that bee away from me.

3. We feel happy whenever we can see our grandmother.

   We feel happy whenever we can see our grandmother.

Let's Write! On a separate sheet of writing paper, write about what a cat found when it sneaked a peek inside a paper bag.

Page 18

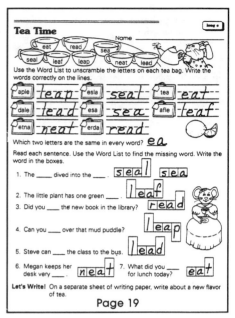

Tea Time
long e

Name _____

eat   read   sea   seal   leaf   leap   neat   lead

Use the Word List to unscramble the letters on each tea bag. Write the words correctly on the lines.

aple — leap   esla — seal   tea — eat
dale — lead   esa — sea   afle — leaf
etna — neat   erda — read

Which two letters are the same in every word? ea

Read each sentence. Use the Word List to find the missing word. Write the word in the boxes.

1. The ___ dived into the ___.   seal   sea
2. The little plant has one green ___.   leaf
3. Did you ___ the new book in the library?   read
4. Can you ___ over that mud puddle?   leap
5. Steve can ___ the class to the bus.   lead
6. Megan keeps her desk very ___   neat
7. What did you ___ for lunch today?   eat

Let's Write! On a separate sheet of writing paper, write about a new flavor of tea.

Page 19

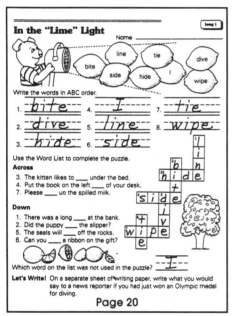

In the "Lime" Light
long i

Name _____

bite   line   tie   dive   side   hide   I   wipe

Write the words in ABC order.

1. bite   4. I   7. tie
2. dive   5. line   8. wipe
3. hide   6. side

Use the Word List to complete the puzzle.

Across
3. The kitten likes to ___ under the bed.
4. Put the book on the left ___ of your desk.
7. Please ___ up the spilled milk.

Down
1. There was a long ___ at the bank.
2. Did the puppy ___ the slipper?
5. The seals will ___ off the rocks.
6. Can you ___ a ribbon on the gift?

Which word on the list was not used in the puzzle? I

Let's Write! On a separate sheet of writing paper, write what you would say to a news reporter if you had just won an Olympic medal for diving.

Page 20

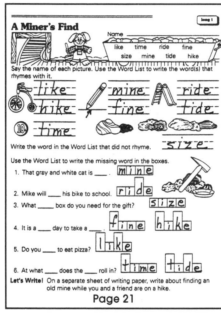

A Miner's Find
long i

Name _____

like   time   ride   fine   size   mine   tide   hike

Say the name of each picture. Use the Word List to write the word(s) that rhymes with it.

like   mine   ride
hike   fine   tide
time

Write the word in the Word List that did not rhyme.   size

Use the Word List to write the missing word in the boxes.

1. That gray and white cat is ___   mine
2. Mike will ___ his bike to school.   ride
3. What ___ box do you need for the gift?   size
4. It is a ___ day to take a ___.   fine   hike
5. Do you ___ to eat pizza?   like
6. At what ___ does the ___ roll in?   time   tide

Let's Write! On a separate sheet of writing paper, write about finding an old mine while you and a friend are on a hike.

Page 21

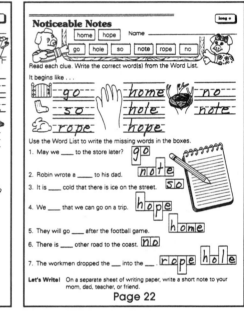

Noticeable Notes
long o

Name _____

home   hope   go   hole   so   note   rope   no

Read each clue. Write the correct word(s) from the Word List. It begins like . . .

go   home   no
so   hole   note
rope   hope

Use the Word List to write the missing words in the boxes.

1. May we ___ to the store later?   go
2. Robin wrote a ___ to his dad.   note
3. It is ___ cold that there is ice on the street.   so
4. We ___ that we can go on a trip.   hope
5. They will go ___ after the football game.   home
6. There is ___ other road to the coast.   no
7. The workmen dropped the ___ into the ___.   rope   hole

Let's Write! On a separate sheet of writing paper, write a short note to your mom, dad, teacher, or friend.

Page 22

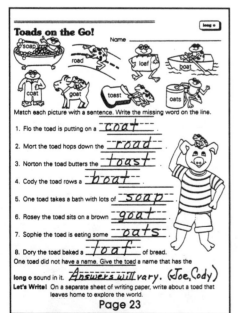

Toads on the Go!
long o

Name _____

soap   road   loaf   boat   coat   goat   toast   oats

Match each picture with a sentence. Write the missing word on the line.

1. Flo the toad is putting on a   coat
2. Mort the toad hops down the   road
3. Norton the toad butters the   toast
4. Cody the toad rows a   boat
5. One toad takes a bath with lots of   soap
6. Rosey the toad sits on a brown   goat
7. Sophie the toad is eating some   oats
8. Dory the toad baked a   loaf   of bread.

One toad did not have a name. Give the toad a name that has the long o sound in it.   Answers will vary. (Joe, Cody)

Let's Write! On a separate sheet of writing paper, write about a toad that leaves home to explore the world.

Page 23

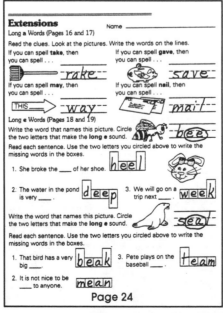

Extensions

Long a Words (Pages 16 and 17)

Name _____

Read the clues. Look at the pictures. Write the words on the lines.

If you can spell **take**, then you can spell . . .   rake
If you can spell **gave**, then you can spell . . .   save
If you can spell **may**, then you can spell . . .   way
If you can spell **nail**, then you can spell . . .   mail

Long e Words (Pages 18 and 19)

Write the word that names this picture. Circle the two letters that make the **long e** sound.   bee

Read each sentence. Use the two letters you circled above to write the missing words in the boxes.

1. She broke the ___ of her shoe.   heel
2. The water in the pond is very ___.   deep
3. We will go on a trip next ___.   week

Write the word that names this picture. Circle the two letters that make the **long e** sound.   seal

Read each sentence. Use the two letters you circled above to write the missing words in the boxes.

1. That bird has a very big ___.   beak
2. It is not nice to be ___ to anyone.   mean
3. Pete plays on the baseball ___.   team

Page 24

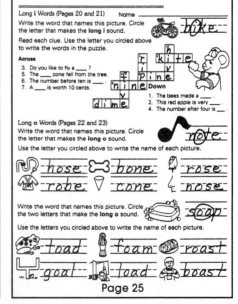

Long i Words (Pages 20 and 21)

Name _____

Write the word that names this picture. Circle the letter that makes the **long i** sound.   bike

Read each clue. Use the letter you circled above to write the words in the puzzle.

Across
3. Do you like to fly a ___ ?
5. The ___ cone fell from the tree.
6. The number before ten is ___.
7. A ___ is worth 10 cents.

kite   pine   nine   dime

Down
1. The bees made a ___.
2. This red apple is very ___.
4. The number after four is ___.

Long o Words (Pages 22 and 23)

Write the word that names this picture. Circle the letter that makes the **long o** sound.   note

Use the letter you circled above to write the name of each picture.

hose   bone   rose
robe   cone   nose

Write the word that names this picture. Circle the two letters that make the **long o** sound.   soap

Use the letters you circled above to write the name of each picture.

toad   foam   roast
goat   toad   boast

Page 25

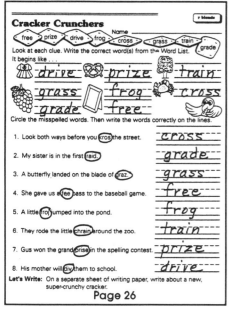

Cracker Crunchers
r blends

Name _____

free · prize · drive · frog · cross · grass · train · grade

Look at each clue. Write the correct word(s) from the Word List. It begins like . . .

drive · prize · train
grass · frog · cross
grade · free

Circle the misspelled words. Then write the words correctly on the lines.

1. Look both ways before you (cros) the street. — cross
2. My sister is in the first (graid). — grade
3. A butterfly landed on the blade of (graz). — grass
4. She gave us a (fee) pass to the baseball game. — free
5. A little (frog) jumped into the pond. — frog
6. They rode the little (chrain) around the zoo. — train
7. Gus won the grand (prise) in the spelling contest. — prize
8. His mother will (driv) them to school. — drive

Let's Write: On a separate sheet of writing paper, write about a new, super-crunchy cracker.

Page 26

Fluffy Flapjacks
l blends

Name _____

plus · plane · fly · float · glide · clap · place · flat

Use the Word List to unscramble the letters on each flapjack. Write the words correctly in the boxes.

float (toalf) · glide (eildg) · plane (aenlp)
place (cpea) · flat (tlaf) · fly (ylf) · plus (ups) · clap (calp)

Use the Word List to write the missing words on the lines.

1. Two p l u s two will equal four.
2. A toy boat will f l o a t in the pond.
3. Glen's bike has a f l a t tire.
4. The little bird cannot f l y yet.
5. Our new sled will g l i d e down the hill.
6. They waited for the p l a n e to land.
7. We can c l a p along while they sing the song.
8. This is the best p l a c e to eat tacos.

Let's Write! On a separate sheet of writing paper, write about the fluffiest flapjack in the world.

Page 27

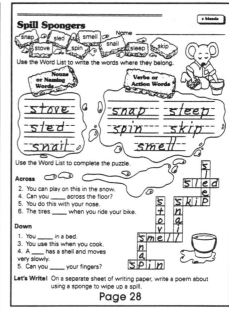

Spill Spongers
s blends

Name _____

snap · sled · smell · stove · spin · snail · sleep · skip

Use the Word List to write the words where they belong.

Nouns or Naming Words
stove · sled · snail

Verbs or Action Words
snap · sleep · spin · skip · smell

Use the Word List to complete the puzzle.

Across
2. You can play on this in the snow.
4. Can you ____ across the floor?
5. You do this with your nose.
6. The tires ____ when you ride your bike.

Down
1. You ____ in a bed.
3. You use this when you cook.
4. A ____ has a shell and moves very slowly.
5. Can you ____ your fingers?

Let's Write! On a separate sheet of writing paper, write a poem about using a sponge to wipe up a spill.

Page 28

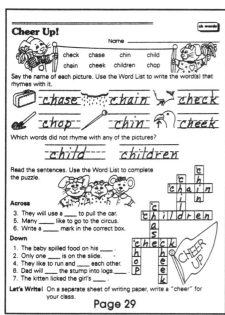

Cheer Up!
ch words

Name _____

check · chase · chin · child · chain · cheek · children · chop

Say the name of each picture. Use the Word List to write the word(s) that rhymes with it.

chase · chain · check
chop · chin · cheek

Which words did not rhyme with any of the pictures?

child · children

Read the sentences. Use the Word List to complete the puzzle.

Across
3. They will use a ____ to pull the car.
5. Many ____ like to go to the circus.
6. Write a ____ mark in the correct box.

Down
1. The baby spilled food on his ____.
2. Only one ____ is on the slide.
3. They like to run and ____ each other.
4. Dad will ____ the stump into logs.
7. The kitten licked the girl's ____.

Let's Write! On a separate sheet of writing paper, write a "cheer" for your class.

Page 29

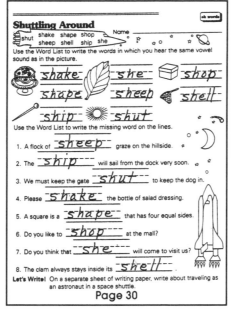

Shuttling Around
sh words

Name _____

shut · shake · shape · shop · sheep · shell · ship · she

Use the Word List to write the words in which you hear the same vowel sound as in the picture.

shake · she · shop
shape · sheep · shell
ship · shut

Use the Word List to write the missing word on the lines.

1. A flock of sheep graze on the hillside.
2. The ship will sail from the dock very soon.
3. We must keep the gate shut to keep the dog in.
4. Please shake the bottle of salad dressing.
5. A square is a shape that has four equal sides.
6. Do you like to shop at the mall?
7. Do you think that she will come to visit us?
8. The clam always stays inside its shell.

Let's Write! On a separate sheet of writing paper, write about traveling as an astronaut in a space shuttle.

Page 30

Whistle a Tune
wh words

Name _____

which · whip · whale · why · where · when · what · wheel

Use the Word List to write the words that ask questions in the boxes.

where · which · why · what · when

Use the Word List to find the words that name things. Write them in the boxes.
wheel · whale · whip

Read each sentence. Use the Word List to write the missing words.

1. When are we going this afternoon?
2. Which red dress will Wendy buy?
3. A huge whale swam near the shore.
4. When are they going to the basketball game?
5. The shopping cart has a broken wheel.
6. What will we see at the zoo?
7. Leon sat down when his trainer snapped the whip.
8. Why is Mother Duck taking her ducklings to the pond?

Some answers can vary.

Let's Write! On a separate sheet of writing paper, write a poem about whistles or whistling.

Page 31

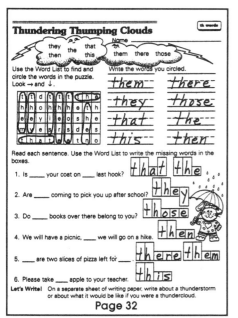

Thundering Thumping Clouds
th words

Name _____

they · the · that · then · this · them · there · those

Use the Word List to find and circle the words in the puzzle. Look → and ↓.

Write the words you circled.
them · there
they · those
that · the
this · then

Read each sentence. Use the Word List to write the missing words in the boxes.

1. Is ____ your coat on ____ last hook? — that, the
2. Are ____ coming to pick you up after school? — they
3. Do ____ books over there belong to you? — those
4. We will have a picnic, ____ we will go on a hike. — then
5. ____ are two slices of pizza left for ____. — there, them
6. Please take ____ apple to your teacher. — this

Let's Write! On a separate sheet of writing paper, write about a thunderstorm or about what it would be like if you were a thundercloud.

Page 32

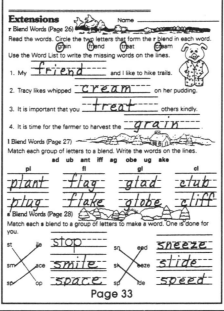

Extensions

Name _____

r Blend Words (Page 26)
Read the words. Circle the two letters that form the r blend in each word.
(gr)ain · (fr)iend · (tr)eat · (cr)eam

Use the Word List to write the missing words on the lines.

1. My friend and I like to hike trails.
2. Tracy likes whipped cream on her pudding.
3. It is important that you treat others kindly.
4. It is time for the farmer to harvest the grain.

l Blend Words (Page 27)
Match each group of letters to a blend. Write the words on the lines.

ad · ub · ant · iff · ag · obe · ug · ake

pl	fl	gl	cl
plant	flag	glad	club
plug	flake	globe	cliff

s Blend Words (Page 28)
Match each s blend to a group of letters to make a word. One is done for you.

st — ile → stop
sm — ace → smile
sp — op → space
sn — eed → sneeze
sl — eeze → slide
sk — ide → speed

Page 33

ch and sh Words (Pages 29 and 30)

Name _____

Read the words.
chick · shed · shark · champ · chime · shine · shave · chair

Write the words that make the sound you hear at the beginning of ☆.
shark · shed · shine · shave

Write the words that make the sound you hear at the beginning of √.
chick · champ · chime · chair

wh and th Words (Pages 31 and 32)
Match each group of letters to the th or wh letters. Write the words on the lines.
orn · ick · ank · ile · iskers · eat · isper · ink

wh	th
whiskers	thorn
wheat	thick
whisper	think
white	thank

Page 34

IF5083 Spelling

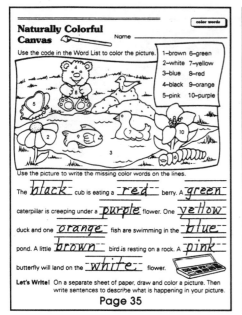

Naturally Colorful Canvas

color words

Name _____

Use the code in the Word List to color the picture.

Word List	
1—brown	6—green
2—white	7—yellow
3—blue	8—red
4—black	9—orange
5—pink	10—purple

Use the picture to write the missing color words on the lines.

The _black_ cub is eating a _red_ berry. A _green_ caterpillar is creeping under a _purple_ flower. One _yellow_ duck and one _orange_ fish are swimming in the _blue_ pond. A little _brown_ bird is resting on a rock. A _pink_ butterfly will land on the _white_ flower.

Let's Write! On a separate sheet of paper, draw and color a picture. Then write sentences to describe what is happening in your picture.

Page 35

Now, on the Count of . . .

number words

Name _____

Trace each number and write its number word next to it.

one two three four five six seven eight nine ten

3 _three_
7 _seven_
5 _five_   4 _four_   8 _eight_
2 _two_   6 _six_   10 _ten_
9 _nine_   1 _one_

Work the problems. Write the answers on the lines. Then write the answers using the correct number words in the puzzle.

Across
1. 3 + 2 = _5_
2. 4 + 2 = _6_
3. 2 + 1 = _3_
4. 1 + 0 = _1_
5. 5 + 3 = _8_
7. 2 + 5 = _7_

Down
1. 2 + 2 = _4_
2. 4 + 3 = _7_
3. 0 + 2 = _2_
6. 4 + 6 = _10_

Crossword answers: five, four, six, three, two, one, eight, nine

Let's Write! On a separate sheet of writing paper, write a math problem using three or more number words.

Page 36

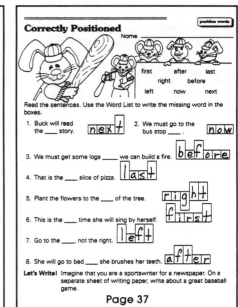

Correctly Positioned

position words

Name _____

Word List		
first	after	last
right	before	
left	now	next

Read the sentences. Use the Word List to write the missing word in the boxes.

1. Buck will read the ___ story. _next_
2. We must go to the bus stop ___. _now_
3. We must get some logs ___ we can build a fire. _before_
4. That is the ___ slice of pizza. _last_
5. Plant the flowers to the ___ of the tree. _right_
6. This is the ___ time she will sing by herself. _first_
7. Go to the ___, not the right. _left_
8. She will go to bed ___ she brushes her teeth. _after_

Let's Write! Imagine that you are a sportswriter for a newspaper. On a separate sheet of writing paper, write about a great baseball game.

Page 37

It's in Sight!

frequently misspelled words

Name _____

Word List		
are	to	you
said	was	of
	goes	have

Write the words in ABC order.

1. _are_   4. _of_   7. _was_
2. _goes_   5. _said_   8. _you_
3. _have_   6. _to_

Write the missing words on the lines. Use the numbered letters to solve the code.

1. The class will be at the farm most _o f_ the day.
2. Andy and Amy _h a v e_ three kittens.
3. Grandmother sent a letter _t o_ Shane.
4. Jan and Donna _a r e_ going to the horse show.
5. Sam _s a i d_ that he can play the drums.
6. She _g o e s_ to the lake every summer.
7. Do _y o u_ like to go camping in the forest?
8. The puppy _w a s_ asleep in the basket.

Great! you did it right!

Let's Write! On a separate sheet of writing paper, write about the most beautiful sight you have ever seen.

Page 38

Take Note of These Words

frequently misspelled words

Name _____

Word List		
come	look	good
my	her	will
	for	all

Use the Word List to unscramble the letters on each pencil. Write the words on the lines.

- rhe → _her_
- rof → _for_
- ym → _my_
- lal → _all_
- dogo → _good_
- loko → _look_
- omce → _come_
- lilw → _will_

Use the Word List to write the missing word on the lines.

1. Did you have a _good_ time at the party?
2. They _will_ help rake the grass.
3. Ted and Jack will _come_ here later.
4. Amy is happy that _her_ grandmother is coming to visit.
5. Did you remember to _look_ for your lost coat?
6. Will _all_ of those boxes fit in the car?
7. This letter is _for_ you.
8. Those are _my_ glasses on the desk.

Let's Write! On a separate sheet of writing paper, write about something that is important to you.

Page 39

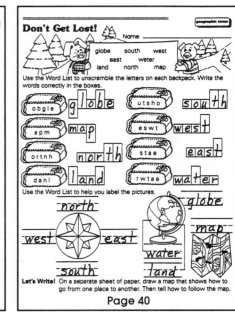

Don't Get Lost!

geographic terms

Name _____

Word List		
globe	south	west
	east	water
	land	north	map

Use the Word List to unscramble the letters on each backpack. Write the words correctly in the boxes.

- obgle → _globe_
- apm → _map_
- ortnh → _north_
- danl → _land_
- utsho → _south_
- eswt → _west_
- stae → _east_
- rwtae → _water_

Use the Word List to help you label the pictures.

north
west   _east_
south

globe
map
water
land

Let's Write! On a separate sheet of paper, draw a map that shows how to go from one place to another. Then tell how to follow the map.

Page 40

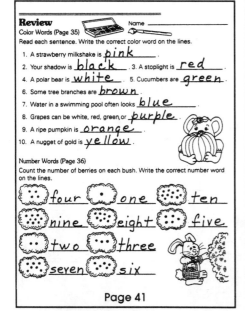

Review

Color Words (Page 35)

Name _____

Read each sentence. Write the correct color word on the lines.

1. A strawberry milkshake is _pink_.
2. Your shadow is _black_.   3. A stoplight is _red_.
4. A polar bear is _white_.   5. Cucumbers are _green_.
6. Some tree branches are _brown_.
7. Water in a swimming pool often looks _blue_.
8. Grapes can be white, red, green, or _purple_.
9. A ripe pumpkin is _orange_.
10. A nugget of gold is _yellow_.

Number Words (Page 36)

Count the number of berries on each bush. Write the correct number word on the lines.

four   _one_   _ten_
nine   _eight_   _five_
two   _three_
seven   _six_

Page 41

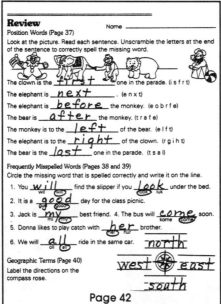

Review

Position Words (Page 37)

Name _____

Look at the picture. Read each sentence. Unscramble the letters at the end of the sentence to correctly spell the missing word.

The clown is the _first_ one in the parade. (i s f r t)
The elephant is _next_. (e n x t)
The elephant is _before_ the monkey. (e o b r f e)
The bear is _after_ the monkey. (t r a f e)
The monkey is to the _left_ of the bear. (e l f t)
The elephant is to the _right_ of the clown. (r g i h t)
The bear is the _last_ one in the parade. (t s a l)

Frequently Misspelled Words (Pages 38 and 39)

Circle the missing word that is spelled correctly and write it on the line.

1. You _look_ find the slipper if you ___ under the bed.
2. It is a _good_ day for the class picnic.
3. Jack is _my_ best friend.   4. The bus will _come_ soon.
5. Donna likes to play catch with _her_ brother.
6. We will _all_ ride in the same car.

Geographic Terms (Page 40)

Label the directions on the compass rose.

north
west   _east_
south

Page 42

A+ SPELLING